GRÉGOIRE SOLOTAREFF

FATHER
CHRISTMAS

THE TRUTH

MACMILLAN

For Didi

absent-minded : Father Christmas can be absent-minded. Once he went ski-ing without his skis. He didn't get far.

accident : one year, Father Christmas had a sleigh-accident. Christmas was cancelled.

acrobat : as a child, Father Christmas wanted to be an acrobat. This was good training for balancing on roofs.

act : when the elves have to act quickly, they wish they had a car.

adult : is Father Christmas an adult? It's hard to tell sometimes.

aeroplane : when he flies his aeroplane, Father Christmas seems happy. But who can tell if he is really happy?

alarm clock : Father Christmas has a very special alarm clock, which tells him exactly when to get up to deliver the presents.

amused : once, when Father Christmas was running around naked in the snow, he fell over. He was not amused.

angel : every Christmas, Father Christmas passes several angels in the sky. Every Christmas, he asks himself if he is seeing things.

artichoke : artichokes have nothing at all to do with Father Christmas. They do not make good presents.

attention : if you ever see a minibus full of Father Christmases, pay no attention to them. They can't be real because there is only one Father Christmas.

baby : Father Christmas has had no experience of dealing with crying babies.

bandit : some bandits look a bit like Father Christmas, but it's easy to tell the difference. Father Christmas would never carry a gun.

battle : when the elves argue, Father Christmas leaves them to battle it out.

beautiful : Father Christmas thinks that his moustache is beautiful. Perhaps that's why some of his presents look a little like him.

bed : Father Christmas's bed isn't all that special.

bee : Father Christmas's bees make sweets, rather than honey.

believe : all Father Christmas's elves believe in him.

bicycle : if you see a red bicycle with white handlebars and white wheels, it could be Father Christmas's.

bird : birds who dress up as Father Christmas always look pretty unconvincing.

black : some of Father Christmas's elves have beards; others don't. Some are black; others aren't. Some are both bearded and black.

blood : Father Christmas likes everything that is red, except his own blood. He faints when he cuts himself.

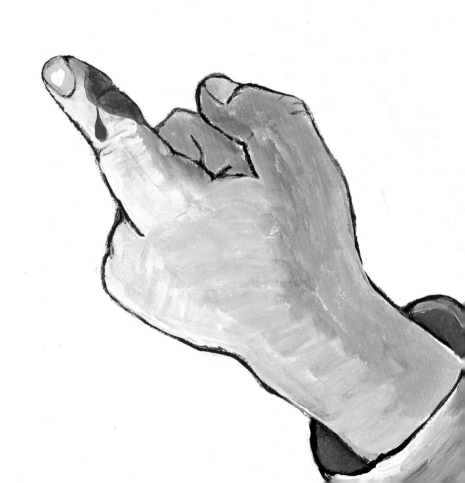

boot : Father Christmas can never resist a new pair of boots.

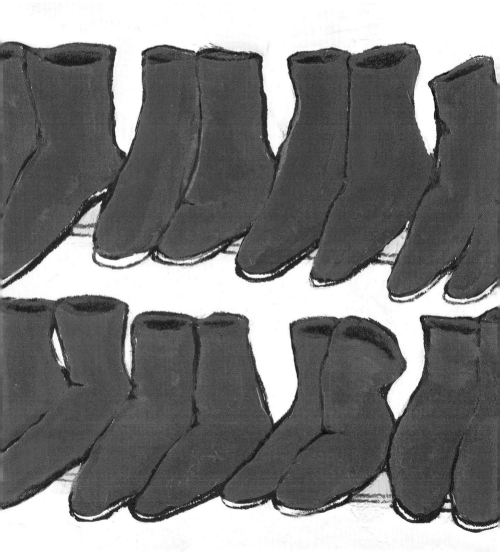

bottom : you must never show your bottom to Father Christmas. Father Christmas refuses to give presents to people or animals who are so rude.

bouquet : if you want to make Father Christmas really happy, put a bouquet of flowers near the chimney on Christmas Eve. Make sure that they are red flowers.

bread : Father Christmas loves bread. He always keeps a loaf of bread and his slippers by the side of his bed, just in case he needs them in the middle of the night.

brother : Father Christmas has a younger brother. He looks very like Father Christmas, but is an altogether more dubious character.

brush : how does Father Christmas manage to brush his moustache and beard at the same time? No one knows.

camping : sometimes Father Christmas goes camping. Then he remembers how boring it is.

cannon : long ago, the elves invented a cannon for long-range present delivery, but Father Christmas has never actually used it.

catastrophe : Father Christmas has never fallen from his sleigh. If he ever did, it would be a catastrophe.

class : when the elves are naughty in class, Father Christmas says he'll call the headmaster. This doesn't bother the elves: they know he *is* the headmaster.

clothes : sometimes it looks as if Father Christmas is wearing a dress or a skirt. In fact, he never wears women's clothes. He wears a tunic.

comfortable : Father Christmas has an old pair of comfortable yellow shoes, but the elves don't think they're very Christmassy, so he never wears them.

confuse : when they don't want to work, the elves disguise themselves as toadstools to confuse Father Christmas. Father Christmas always leaves toadstools alone: he knows they are poisonous. So are elves.

connoisseur : Father Christmas is a connoisseur of both armchairs and sleighs.

crocodile : sometimes crocodiles try to look friendly, hoping that Father Christmas will visit them. Sadly, he is so busy that crocodiles completely slip his mind.

dangerous : it is very dangerous to shoot arrows into the air, especially on Christmas Eve. You might hit Father Christmas.

dinghy : in the spring, when the snow melts, the elves travel in dinghies. That way, they keep their feet dry.

disguise : sometimes Father Christmas's reindeer disguise themselves as Christmas trees. It suits them.

distributor : the elves invented an automatic present distributor, but it could not guarantee accurate delivery. Father Christmas has never used it.

doctor : when Father Christmas is ill, he can never get doctors to call on him. They say he lives too far away.

dog : Father Christmas has a dog. She is called 'Beauty'.

doubt : an elf leaves you in no doubt when he's sticking his tongue out at you.

dreadfully : elves can be dreadfully lazy. They will fall asleep any time, anywhere.

dream : Father Christmas dreams of building a little igloo on a beach and going there on holiday.

elf : some of the elves want to look just like Father Christmas, but they know that they can never be as big as he is.

exciting : Father Christmas has only once seen a Christmas butterfly. He found it very exciting.

fall : if the elves fall over when they are playing, they never cry. In fact, elves hardly ever cry.

father : Father Christmas's father is very proud of his son.

flag : Father Christmas's flag is very heavy for the elves to carry around, and serves no useful purpose.

fog : if, one day around Christmas, you peer through the fog and see a red lorry travelling at top speed, it's probably something to do with Father Christmas.

fortunately : fortunately Father Christmas doesn't have a daughter. A wolf could easily take her for Little Red Riding Hood.

four : to make a really convincing Father Christmas snowman, you need four carrots.

goldfish : Father Christmas loves goldfish. Goldfish love him, too.

green : if there were a Father Christmas who visited frogs, he would probably dress in green.

guard : the elves take turns guarding Father Christmas's boots, but they're not very good at it. They always fall asleep.

hair-clip : one night, when Father Christmas was asleep, the elves decided to find out what he would look like with hair-clips in his beard. Luckily, Father Christmas took it as a joke.

hang up : if the 'phone rings and the person on the line says, 'Hello, this is Father Christmas,' hang up immediately. It can't really be Father Christmas, because he doesn't have a 'phone.

helmet : in the Middle Ages, Father Christmas had to wear a helmet to protect himself from enemies.

hide : Father Christmas always knows when someone is hiding something from him.

hide-and-seek : when Father Christmas plays hide-and-seek with his elves, he pretends he's crying, and they run out to comfort him.

hood : Father Christmas looks sinister in a hood. That's why he always wears a hat.

idiot : Father Christmas is shocked when he reads the stories people write about him for children. He thinks the authors are idiots.

impatient : Father Christmas is always impatient for the first snow. He loves Christmas just as much as you do.

impossible : it's impossible to tell what is inside a really well-wrapped present.

incognito : sometimes Father Christmas goes to town incognito. When strangers stop and stare at him, he realizes that people are not so stupid after all.

India : some men in India try to impersonate Father Christmas. The children are not convinced.

Indian : American Indians don't believe Father Christmas exists. They call him 'Big-Red-And-White-Man-Who-Doesn't-Exist'.

invent : the elves don't just invent machines for delivering presents. They have also invented a special contraption for drying Father Christmas's moustache so that it doesn't lose its amusing shape.

irritating : Father Christmas sometimes does stupid things, like sewing his hat to his beard. He finds this very irritating.

jolly : Father Christmas thinks it would be much more jolly if ambulances were painted red on Christmas Eve.

king : once, someone gave Father Christmas a crown. Occasionally he puts it on, but he wouldn't really like to be a king.

late : Father Christmas hates it when the elves are late. If they aren't ready when it's time to leave, that's their tough luck.

letter : Father Christmas sends letters in red envelopes, but they are hardly ever delivered. No one at the post office can read the address.

Little Red Riding Hood : when the big bad wolf meets one of Father Christmas's elves, he stops to wonder if it is Little Red Riding Hood who has disguised herself as an elf to avoid being eaten. Then he eats the elf.

look : some of the elves don't look like Father Christmas at all. Others bear a striking resemblance to him.

love : Father Christmas loves all animals, especially really ugly ones.

luck : Father Christmas does not believe in the Loch Ness Monster. This is hard luck on the monster.

make fun : Easter bunnies sometimes make fun of Father Christmas. But they're just silly. There's nothing to laugh about.

medal : in the olden days, really well-behaved children used to be given a medal with Father Christmas's picture on it. It has been years since a child last got one.

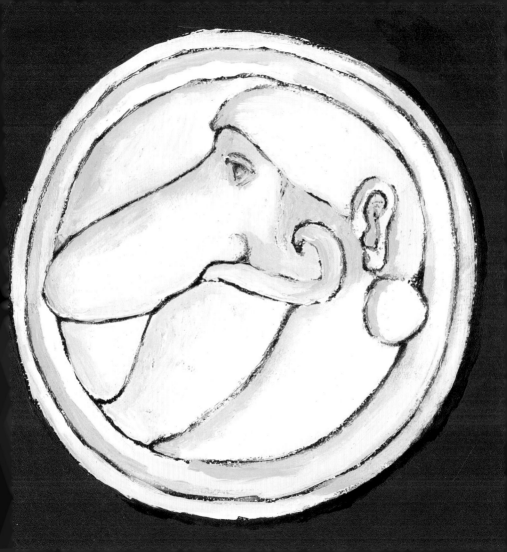

medium-sized : Father Christmas describes his nose as medium-sized.

mischievous : some elves are more mischievous than others.

miserable : when he was little, Father Christmas was miserable, because Father Christmas hadn't been invented yet.

Morocco : some old men in Morocco look remarkably like Father Christmas.

mummy : sometimes the smallest elves call Father Christmas 'mummy' by mistake. He doesn't mind.

nap : Father Christmas often takes a nap in the cradle he had when he was a child. He is still very fond of it.

neat : Father Christmas wears his hair in a neat plait down his back. Not a lot of people know that.

night : at night, Father Christmas sometimes dreams he is a child opening presents.

nightmare : very occasionally Father Christmas has scary nightmares, just like everyone else.

no good : Father Christmas is no good at painting. His pictures are just scribbles.

nothing : even when Father Christmas seems to be doing nothing, he is usually thinking of ideas for presents.

obedient : Father Christmas always makes a fuss of the most obedient elves.

old : some of Father Christmas's reindeer are too old to pull his sleigh. This makes them a little sad, but they have very happy memories.

ostrich : in Africa, where it is far too hot for reindeer, Father Christmas has to ride an ostrich. He always feels rather nervous about it. So does the ostrich.

painting : Father Christmas loves painting. He thinks he's rather good at it.

parent : elves don't have parents, which means that Father Christmas has to look after them particularly well, especially when they are little.

passion : Father Christmas has a passion for sailing. The elves don't like it much, but they follow Father Christmas everywhere.

peace : Father Christmas would love to go for a ride on his own now and then. Sadly, his elves never give him a minute's peace.

peculiar : Father Christmas likes wearing yellow slippers. The elves think this is very peculiar.

plate : all the elves are envious of Father Christmas's plate. Theirs are much smaller.

pointed : Father Christmas has pointed feet. That's why his boots are pointed.

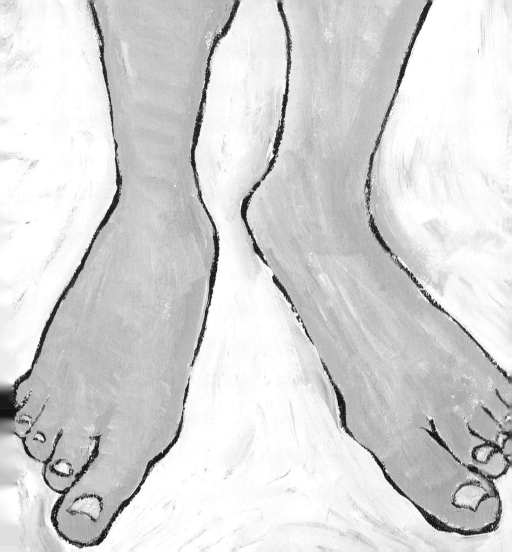

ponder : Father Christmas often stops work to ponder for a while, and why not?

portrait : Father Christmas would love to have his portrait painted. Sadly, this will never happen, because he can never be seen by anyone, not even an artist.

Portugal : when he is travelling round the world on Christmas Eve, Father Christmas always stops off in Portugal for a quick picnic.

prepare : Father Christmas prepares carefully for his trips. He even has special boots for hot climates.

quilt : one Christmas, the elves gave Father Christmas a lovely new quilt but it was a bit big for him.

radish : radishes are Father Christmas's favourite vegetable.

rainbow : often Father Christmas
only narrowly avoids collision
with rainbows.

recognizable : Father Christmas is easily recognizable, even from behind.

reluctant : when the cheekier elves tell Father Christmas that he looks like an elephant dressed in red, he is reluctantly forced to agree.

ride : Father Christmas's dog has a good friend who is so big that Father Christmas can ride on his back. The dog doesn't enjoy it much, though, so Father Christmas never stays on long.

rocket : it would be easier for Father Christmas to travel round the whole world on Christmas Eve if he had a rocket, but it would make the reindeer awfully sad.

sad : occasionally, Father Christmas is sad. No one knows why.

signature : Father Christmas's signature is so complicated that no one can forge it.

silly : when an elf is silly and sulky, Father Christmas has to punish him. This doesn't help: the elf just goes on sulking.

sleigh : Father Christmas has a luxury sleigh, but he thinks it's a little too flashy, so he just uses his ordinary one.

solitude : Father Christmas likes a bit of solitude now and then. It gives him time to make plans for the future.

steam : Father Christmas has such hot baths that the elves can hardly see him through the steam.

stork : storks sometimes claim to have seen Father Christmas, but they are lying.

submarine : Father Christmas doesn't use his submarine for work: just for pleasure.

summer : Father Christmas has completely different clothes for winter and summer. But then, so do you.

sunburnt : in Spain it is sometimes so hot that the reindeer refuse to pull the sleigh, and Father Christmas has to use donkeys. But they go so slowly that Father Christmas always gets sunburnt.

tedious : Father Christmas's elves like fooling around so much that it can become tedious.

tired : Father Christmas gets tired sometimes, which isn't surprising, given how hard he works.

toy : Father Christmas personally tests all the toys he makes, but he gives them to children even if they don't work. After all, a toy that doesn't work is better than nothing.

train : sometimes, on his travels, Father Christmas tries to train bad dogs, but he never has time to do it properly.

unhappy : every year the bears' hopes for a visit from Father Christmas are dashed. This makes them very unhappy.

unicorn : the Christmas unicorn is like the Christmas zebra. It's an ordinary unicorn, but it is red, and it doesn't exist.

unlike : Father Christmas doesn't like dancing and isn't very good at it, unlike his elves.

unrecognizable : if he shaved his beard off, Father Christmas would be unrecognizable, and would probably frighten the elves.

urgent : when the elves have urgent business to see to, they travel by minibus.

use : Father Christmas's car is very old, but that doesn't matter, as he doesn't use it much.

village : Father Christmas doesn't live in a house. He lives in the elves' village. He stays with each elf for a week at a time so that the other elves don't get jealous.

violin : when Father Christmas plays the violin, his nose always gets in the way. It's sad because, had he not been Father Christmas, he would have liked to have been a violinist.

wagon : one day, for fun, the elves climbed into the wagons at the present factory. They had a terrible accident, which just goes to show that you should never do things like that.

wait up : it's completely pointless waiting up for Father Christmas in the hope of seeing him. Nobody has ever seen him.

wake up : Father Christmas doesn't like waking up in the morning. The elves try to make it easier for him by bringing him a cup of tea.

wing : if Father Christmas had wings, he probably wouldn't need his reindeer.

wonder : sometimes Father Christmas wonders whether he was right to choose the job he has. But nearly all grown-ups wonder that sometimes.

xylophone : Father Christmas calls the elves in to dinner by hitting the red keys on his xylophone. If he makes a mistake the elves don't come.

young : Father Christmas's bright blue eyes make him look much younger than he really is.

zebra : the Christmas zebra is an ordinary zebra, but its stripes are red not black, and it doesn't exist.